SHOULD YOU PUT THEM IN A ZOO?

ANIMAL BOOK FOR 8 YEAR OLDS

Children's Animal Books

Speedy Publishing LLC
40 E. Main St. #1156
Newark, DE 19711
www.speedypublishing.com

Some people say zoos are important as teaching tools and to save endangered species. Other people say zoos are no better than jails for animals. What do you think? Let's find out some more.

Wild Animals

THE STORY
OF ZOOS

There have been zoos for almost as long as people have lived in cities. The oldest zoo we know about was in Egypt, and existed over five thousand years ago. Historians think people kept the animals to amuse their rulers, but also so the rulers could hunt dangerous animals in safer conditions than going out into the wilderness.

Emperor Wen Wang of China founded a zoo as part of the Garden of Intelligence, three thousand years ago. The park covered more than 1,500 acres, and the star attraction was a family of giant pandas.

From around 1100, the kings and queens of England kept a zoo, or *"menagerie"*, of animals otherwise not known in England, like lions and camels. This was partly to amuse the nobility, and partly to impress visitors.

A zoo in Vienna opened in 1752 and is still functioning! The Tiergarten Schonbrunn was at first exclusively for the nobility. In the 1770s it became open to the general public, at no charge.

Zebras.

In the French Revolution, which started in 1789, the system of government by kings and nobles was overthrown, and many of the nobility were executed. The state confiscated their property, including their private collections of rare animals.

The revolutionary government created a zoological garden in Paris to take care of, and display, the animals who had once belonged to the wealthy.

The garden is still functioning. Learn more about the French Revolution in the Baby Professor book *The French Revolution: People Power in Action.*

Tiger in captivity.

In 1847, Andrew Downs established the first zoo in North America, in Halifax, Nova Scotia. It was a vast collection of animals, birds, and plants, and at the time it was the largest collection outside of the zoo in London, England.

After a few years, Downs closed the zoo and sold his collection so he could go to New York to work at the Bronx Zoo. When he got there, though, he found there had been some misunderstanding and there was no job for him!

The first public aquarium was part of the London Zoo. It opened in 1853, and was called The Fish House. From the outside it looked like a greenhouse, but inside there were many different tanks to house and display the different fish species.

When the zoo in Hamburg, Germany, opened in 1907, it was the first zoo to try to house its animals in settings something like what they would have been used to in nature. There were a minimum of fences and cages, and animals like antelopes and giraffes were able to move about in large enclosures. This set a new model for how to take care of zoo animals.

The Association of Zoos and Aquariums was founded in 1924. It establishes guidelines for staff training, facilities, and animal welfare to try to raise the standards of zoos all around the world.

Cute Humboldt Penguins (Spheniscus Humboldt) in a zoo, Japan.

In 1963 the first safari park opened, in Japan. In a traditional zoo, the animals are in enclosures. In a safari park, the animals roam in a wide open area and visitors move among them in enclosed cars or trains.

In 2007, a huge game preserve opened in South Africa. It was the first such facility to offer visitors a chance to see and get close to animals like Elephants, Rhinoceroses, Water Buffalo, Lions, and Leopards in something similar to their natural habitat.

As with a safari park, visitors to game preserves travel in closed vehicles while the animals live and move freely. The game preserve covers many thousands of acres.

Children at zoo feeding Giraffe.

THE ARGUMENT FOR ZOOS

H ere are some of the reasons for having zoos and keeping animals in them:

- When people can go and look at animals for real, and not in a book or on the computer, they can understand and appreciate the animals more. This makes them more likely to protect animals and think about their well-being.

- Some zoos protect animals that are rare or endangered. They keep them in a safe environment where hunters won't kills them. For many animals, their natural habitat is almost gone, so zoos and wildlife preserves are the only places left for them. Read the Baby Professor books Endangered Mammals from Around the World and Vulnerable, Endangered, and Critically Endangered Animals to learn more about threats to animals.

Portrait of male Lowland Gorilla in captivity.

- When animal populations get very low, individual animals can have trouble finding mates. Some zoos have breeding programs that bring individuals together and provides the conditions where they can successfully have babies.

Baby Rhino playing and eating hay in green field.

- Zoos are a worthwhile tradition. A family visiting a zoo can share a positive experience together, outdoors and without staring at computer screens.

- Sometimes people buy an exotic pet, or bring one home from a trip. Then they find they do not want to keep it in their home. Often, a zoo is the only place that will take in such an animal.

Giant Panda in zoo.

THE
ARGUMENT
AGAINST

Here are some reasons not to continue to have zoos:

- Animals in captivity can suffer from stress and boredom, especially those that are used to hunting or migrating over wide areas.

- Because people like to see baby animals, some zoos encourage more babies than their set-up can support. They then sell the surplus animals, to other zoos if they can, but sometimes to circuses or to be slaughtered for their meat or fur.

- Although some zoos try to introduce animals born in the zoo back into the wild, most do not. The zoo population never gets the experience of life in its native habitat.

- If the zoo exhibits animals captured in the wild, it means there are that many fewer animals able to contribute to the free population. It increases pressure on species that may already be under threat.

Chimpanzee

- Standards for cage size, ventilation, food, water, and health care for zoo animals in most countries are minimal. Animals suffer from inadequate space and other poor conditions.

- Although many larger zoos try to treat their animals well and provide a natural environment for them, many smaller zoos and animal exhibitions do not. The animals may be confined to cages and concrete enclosures, with no chance to live as they would in the wild.

Bear Boredom.

ODD ZOO FACTS

Here are some interesting and strange facts about zoos:

- At the start of World War II, the London Zoos in England killed all its poisonous snakes so the animals would not get loose if the zoo was bombed.

- In 1987, a jaguar got loose at the zoo in Belgrade, now in Serbia. It was going to attack a member of the zoo staff, but a German shepherd guard dog attacked the jaguar and saved the person's life.

- In the 1900s in England, you could pay to gain admission to a certain zoo, or get in for free if you brought a dog or cat they could feed to the lions!

- In 2004, a French zoo sent almost 20 baboons to an English game preserve. The baboons understand certain instructions—but in French only, so the keepers had to learn some French to talk with them.

- China owns the pandas in all the zoos in the world, lending them out for a fee of around one million dollars per year for a pair. The money goes to help conservation efforts in China.

- A man from the Congo named Ota Benga, a member of a pygmy tribe, was exhibited in the U.S. as a zoo creature in the early 1900s. Around the same time, Paris, France had a whole zoo of people from tribes around the world, from Madagascar and China to Tunisia and the Sudan. Millions of people visited the exhibition.

- In World War II in Japan, there was nothing with which to feed the elephants at the Tokyo zoo. They went on performing the tricks they had learned in a heartbreaking attempt to convince their keepers to feed them.

- Zoos accept used Christmas trees after families are done with them. They use the trees to feed some of the animals.

Elephant behind bars.

- When two of their popular animals died in a zoo in Palestine in 2009, the zoo staff painted two donkeys with black and white stripes and put them in the zebra enclosure to replace the dead zebras.

- Some thieves wanted to steal a koala from a zoo in Australia in 2006. The koala fought back so hard, scratching their faces and arms, that the thieves gave up. They stole a crocodile instead!

Elephant in the zoo.

LOVING THE ANIMALS OF OUR WORLD

Whether they are in captivity or in the wild, animals share this planet with us. They deserve our love and respect, and as we study them we may discover many things about ourselves. Learn more about animals and how they live in Baby Professor books like *The Great White Shark, Who Lives in the Barren Desert? The World's Most Beautiful Birds!* and *How do Animals Help the Forest Grow?*

Visit
BABY PROFESSOR
EDUCATION KIDS
www.BabyProfessorBooks.com
to download Free Baby Professor eBooks
and view our catalog of new and exciting
Children's Books